U.S. Military Forces

U.S. SPECIAL OPS FORCES

LUKE COLINS

BLACK RABBIT BOOKS

Bolt is published by Black Rabbit Books
P.O. Box 3263, Mankato, Minnesota, 56002.
www.blackrabbitbooks.com

Jennifer Besel, editor; Michael Sellner, interior designer; Catherine Cates, cover designer; Omay Ayres, photo researcher

Library of Congress Cataloging-in-Publication Data
Names: Colins, Luke, author.
Title: U.S. Special Ops forces / by Luke Colins.
Description: Mankato, Minnesota : Black Rabbit Books, [2021]
Series: Bolt. U.S. Military Forces | Includes bibliographical references and index.
Audience: Ages 8-12 | Audience: Grades 4-6
Summary: "Learn about U.S. special operations forces, including the missions they do and the powerful soldiers who make up the Green Berets, Army Rangers, Navy SEALs, and other teams."— Provided by publisher.
Identifiers: LCCN 2019040255 (print) | LCCN 2019040256 (ebook)
ISBN 9781623103019 (hardcover) | ISBN 9781644663974 (paperback)
ISBN 9781623103958 (ebook)
Subjects: LCSH: Special forces (Military science)—United States—Juvenile literature. | Special operations (Military science)—United States—Juvenile literature.
Classification: LCC UA34.S64 C64 2021 (print) | LCC UA34.S64 (ebook)
DDC 356/.160973—dc23
LC record available at https://lccn.loc.gov/2019040255
LC ebook record available at https://lccn.loc.gov/2019040256

Image Credits

1stmardiv.marines.mil: Lance Cpl. Tyler Reiriz/U.S. Marine Corps, 27 (b); af.mil: 2nd Lt. Kay M. Nissen/U.S. Air Force, 20–21 (Ghostrider); Osakabe Yasuo/U.S. Air Force, 6 (b); Senior Airman Justyn M. Freeman/U.S. Air Force, 19; Alamy: devilmaya, 16 (compass); americanspecialops.com: Petty Officer 1st Class Elisandro T. Diaz/U.S. Navy, 26; army.mil: Spc. Steven Hitchcock/U.S. Army, 28–29; commons.wikimedia.org: Airwolfhound, 20–21 (Osprey); Dybdal, 17 (weapon); Senior Chief Mass Communication Specialist Andrew McKaskle/U.S. Navy, 24–25; defense.gov: U.S. Air Force, 18; Dreamstime: Ultraone, 16 (helmet), 17 (vest); federalresources.com: Federal Resources, 17 (radio); iStock: zabelin, Cover; jbcharleston.jb.mil: A1C James Richardson/U.S. Air Force, 1, 8–9 (bkgd); military.wikia.org: Military Wikia, 13 (machine gun); moody.af.mil: Staff Sgt. Jeremy T. Lock/U.S. Air Force, 4–5; sealswcc.com: SEAL:SWCC, 6 (t), 27 (t); Shutterstock: Alex Kravtsov, 14; ANURAKE SINGTO-ON, 31; CreativeHQ, 16 (goggles); Getmilitaryphotos, 3, 10–11; Katarzyna Mazurowska, 16–17 (bkgd); Militarist, 13 (rifle); Neuevector, Cover (wings); PRESSLAB, 13 (main), 32; santoelia, 17 (explosives); Sergei Gontsarov, 13 (pistol); Tony El-Azzi, 13 (knife); thebalancecareers.com: U.S. Navy, 22–23; Every effort has been made to contact copyright holders for material reproduced in this book. Any omissions will be rectified in subsequent printings if notice is given to the publisher.

Contents

CHAPTER 1

To *Protect* and Serve

All around the world, U.S. special ops forces are secretly doing their jobs. They are gathering information. They are **raiding terrorist** hideouts. They might even be parachuting into enemy **territory**.

Important Roles

Special operations forces are teams of highly trained soldiers. The United States has several different special ops teams. Some are best at attacking enemies on land. Others are trained for air or sea **missions**. But all the forces work to keep the United States safe.

SOME PLACES WHERE U.S. SPECIAL OPS FORCES HAVE WORKED

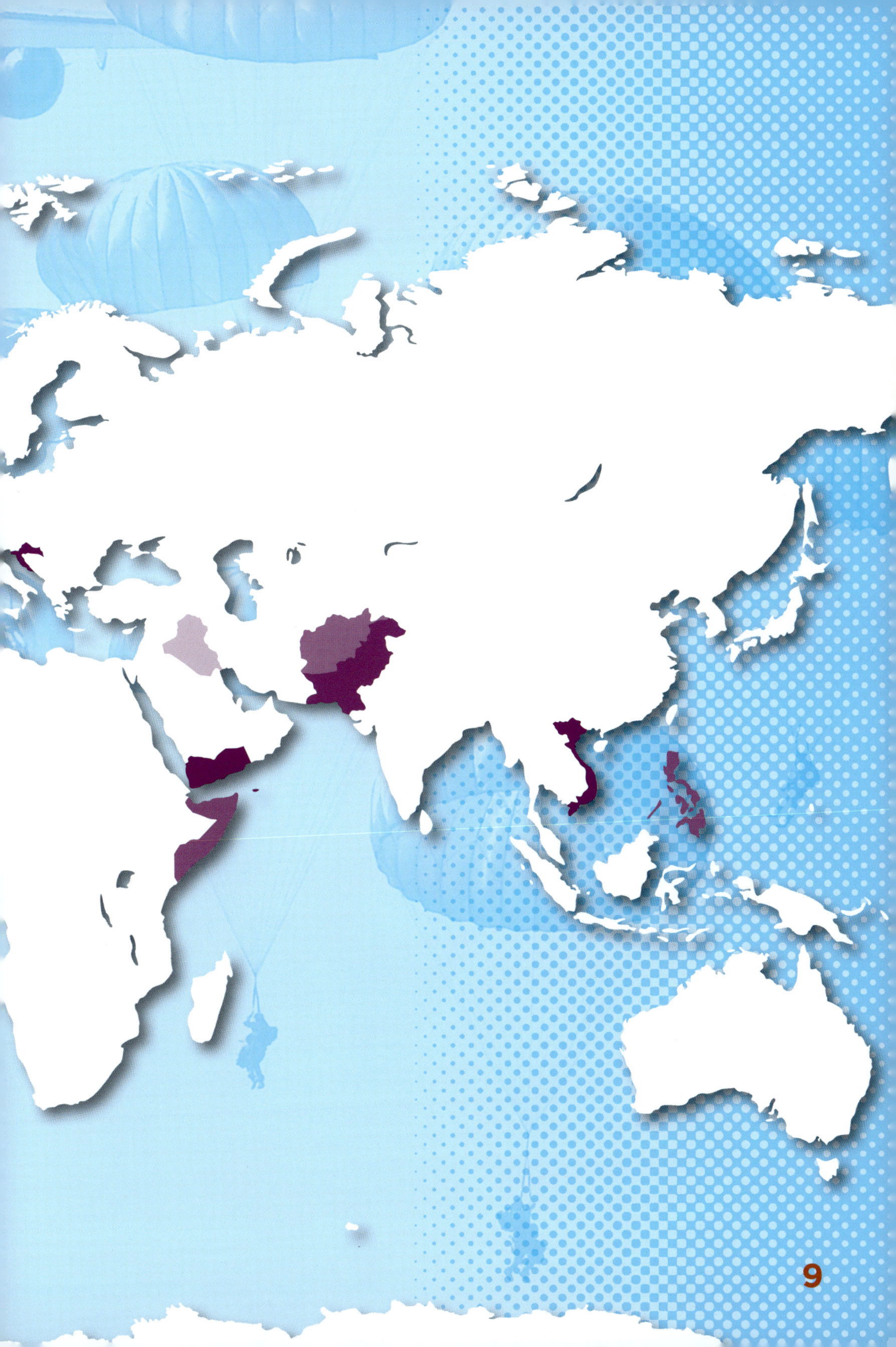

Green Berets is a nickname. The unit's real name is U.S. Army Special Forces.

CHAPTER 2

Land Forces

When quick, secret action is needed, the U.S. government uses special ops forces. Each group is trained to handle different missions.

The U.S. Army's Green Berets fight in small numbers. They practice **guerrilla warfare**. With this type of fighting, the soldiers attack when it's least expected. They use their skills to secretly stop enemy attacks. They also rescue **hostages**.

Army Rangers

The Rangers are another U.S. Army special ops force. Rangers are always ready. They can be anywhere in the world in 18 hours or less. They take over enemy landing strips. They fight terrorists. They also save prisoners of war.

Weapons Used by Army Rangers

rifle

machine gun

pistol

knife

Delta Force

Delta Force is an ultrasecret special ops team. The U.S. government doesn't even admit the group is real. These soldiers go into dangerous places. For some missions, they dress like normal people to blend in. Then they can surprise enemies.

SPECIAL OPS GEAR

HELMETS

NIGHT-VISION GOGGLES

COMPASSES

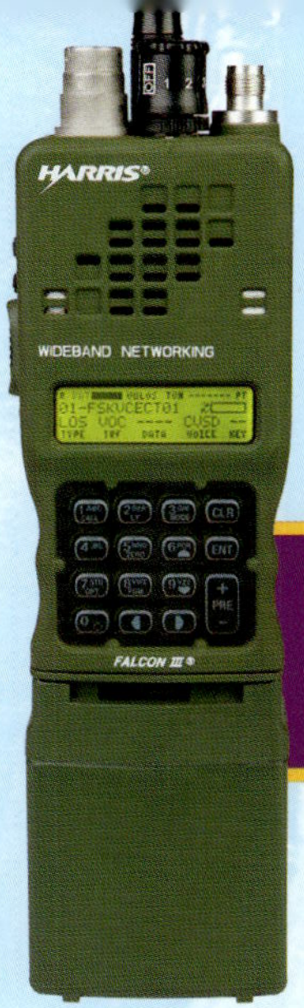

RADIOS

BULLETPROOF VESTS

WEAPONS

EXPLOSIVES

CHAPTER 3

Air and Sea Forces

The U.S. military also has forces that do missions from the air and sea. Air Commandos are part of the Air Force. These soldiers are pararescuers and **combat** controllers. Controllers guide aircraft and lead air attacks. Pararescuers jump from aircraft into dangerous areas. They rescue injured or captured soldiers.

Recruits Who Pass Pararescue Training
about 20%

SOME COMMANDOS' AIRCRAFT

By the Numbers

WINGSPAN
132.6 feet
(40.4 meters)

CV-22 Osprey

WINGSPAN
84.6 feet
(25.8 m)

AC-130J Ghostrider

LENGTH
97.8 feet
(29.8 m)

HEIGHT
39.2 feet
(11.9 m)

LENGTH
57.3 feet
(17.5 m)

HEIGHT
22.1 feet
(6.7 m)

Navy SEALs

U.S. Navy SEALs spend a lot of time in water. They attach **mines** to ships. They also travel underwater to gather information about enemies.

Becoming a SEAL is very hard. The training can last more than 30 months. They learn combat diving and land warfare. In one exercise, they swim with their hands and legs tied up.

SEALs do many water missions. But they are also trained to work on land and in the air. In fact, SEAL stands for sea, air, and land.

SEAL DELIVERY VEHICLE (SDV)

SEAL delivery teams use minisubs. SDVs help soldiers travel underwater.

BATTERY-POWERED

CARRIES
SIX
SEALS
OPERATES
EVEN IF
FLOODED

CHAPTER 4

Different Missions

The U.S. military trains special ops forces to be ready for anything. It has more teams than the ones in this book. Some are highly trained sailors or pilots. Others focus on spy missions.

Other Special Ops Forces

Special Warfare Combatant Craft Crewman (SWCC)
often helps transport SEALs to and from missions

Marine Raiders Regiment
often helps train other countries to fight enemies

160th Special Operations Aviation Regiment (SOAR)
does missions that require soldiers to arrive by air, often at night

Always Prepared

U.S. special ops teams are the best of the best. They are called to do dangerous jobs. But they are trained and ready. These soldiers do all they can to keep the United States safe.

GLOSSARY

combat (kahm-BAT)—active fighting, often in a war

guerrilla warfare (guh-RIL-uh WARW-fair)—sudden, unexpected attacks carried out by small groups

hostage (HAHS-tij)—a person captured by someone else

mine (MYN)—an explosive in the ground or in water that is set to explode when disturbed

mission (MISH-uhn)—a job assigned to a soldier

raid (REYD)—a surprise attack on an enemy by soldiers

territory (TER-uh-tor-ee)—a geographic area belonging to or under the control of a governmental authority

terrorist (TER-ur-ist)—a person who uses violent acts to frighten people in order to achieve a goal

LEARN MORE

BOOKS

Grack, Rachel. *U.S. Special Forces.* Serving Our Country. Mankato, MN: Amicus, 2019.

Noll, Elizabeth. *Special Ops Forces.* Rank It! Mankato, MN: Black Rabbit Books, 2017.

Yomtov, Nel. *Special Ops.* Military Missions. Minneapolis: Bellwether Media, 2017.

WEBSITES

Air Commandos
www.afsoc.af.mil/About-Us/Fact-Sheets/Display/Article/560215/air-commandos/

Train to Become an Elite U.S. Navy SEAL
www.navy.com/node/160?activity=1239969

United States Army Rangers
www.army.mil/ranger/

INDEX